ESSEX

A portrait in colour

———

MARK & ELIZABETH MITCHELS

COUNTRYSIDE BOOKS

Other counties in this series include:

DORSET
HAMPSHIRE
SURREY
SUSSEX

For Our Children

First Published 1992
© Mark & Elizabeth Mitchels 1992

COUNTRYSIDE BOOKS
3 CATHERINE ROAD
NEWBURY, BERKSHIRE

ISBN 1 85306 189 1

Produced through MRM Associates Ltd., Reading
Typeset by Acorn Bookwork, Salisbury, Wilts
Printed in England

Contents

INTRODUCTION

We are what the past has made us, and the same is true of places. Essex as it is today reflects the changes which have occurred over the centuries. Once it was a vast forest, which for a time was the exclusive property of the Norman kings, who used it for hunting and imposed cruel punishments on those who dared to share it with them. The old Roman road thrust up from the south west, passing through Chelmsford and on to Colchester, but otherwise the region was isolated and ignored.

It was only in the 13th century that the woodland clearances began, and the evidence is in the scores of village names which end with field. Finchingfield, for example, recalls the forest clearing owned by the Saxon, Finc. Oak and ash grew in profusion, and were used to construct some of the earliest and finest surviving barns in Europe. Coggeshall Great Barn, Cressing Temple, and Priors' Hall Barn proclaim the magnificent achievements of the carpenters of the medieval period. Stone was hard to find, but the wealth of wood may still be seen in beautiful houses and farmsteads, while the humbler cottages with their simple weatherboarding are a charming feature of the county. Even churches and castles made use of the abundant supply of wood, as may be seen today at Greensted Saxon Church and the reconstructed Mountfitchet Castle. The former glory of the woodlands may be glimpsed in the remnants of Epping and Hatfield Forests.

The rivers were a source of both wealth and danger. They were the highways before the forests gave way to tracks and roads, and towns like Maldon grew rich with each well-laden craft which berthed beside them. The graceful barges which now tie up beside the Hythe continue a maritime link which goes back over a thousand years. But their very wealth enticed less welcome travellers. The Anglo-Saxons and then the Vikings used the Rivers Stour, Blackwater, Crouch and Thames itself to grasp the riches they sought, and could so easily obtain.

Forts were built to defend the vulnerable estuaries whenever they were threatened, and those at Bradwell, Hadleigh and Tilbury remain if only as shadows of their sometime power. When the kingdom of the East Saxons became part of England the trade returned, and right into modern times barges and coastal vessels have tied up at Mistley, Brightlingsea and Wivenhoe and exchanged one cargo for another, with profit and the satisfaction of a well-earned drink on land. The wealth of towns such as Maldon was dependent on the river; when the Blackwater froze over in 1776, two thirds of the town's workforce was unemployed. Many of the smaller river ports have lost their importance, but not so with Harwich, which had the foresight to expand into the international passenger market and which is now the second largest passenger port in Britain, with a renown far exceeding any ordinary town of this size.

The sea has not always shown such favour. We should not forget the devastation caused by flooding. For instance in February 1953 floods caused by high Spring tides together with hurricane force winds overwhelmed the coastal defences from Manningtree to West Ham; 100 people lost their lives and 21,000 were left homeless in the low lying areas such as Harwich, Jaywick, Tilbury, Purfleet and Canvey Island. All down the coast of Essex there are intricate, vastly expensive sea defences which await the test, culminating in the Thames Barrier near Woolwich.

In 1661, the Dutch presented Charles II at his Restoration with *Mary* & the *Bezan*, and a new word, jacht (pronounced 'yacht'), meaning a hunt or chase. Both the King and the Duke of York were highly competitive, and the trend they set made the connection of yachting with competition ever since. Centres such as Burnham on Crouch, 'the Cowes of the East Coast', have prospered and grown in popularity and prestige. For the non-sporting visitor, the benefits of the east coast climate are clear: the Essex Sunshine Coast has the lowest average annual rainfall in Britain, so that resorts such as Clacton-on-Sea and Walton-on-the Naze have a well-earned reputation as ideal spots for a family holiday.

Colchester is proud to be Britain's oldest recorded town, and thrives on the memory of the terrible day in AD 60 when Boudicca's tribesmen destroyed it with fire and sword. The Castle Museum has a chilling evocation of the event, heightened by the knowledge that the events took place on the site itself. Over the centuries the fortunes of Saffron Walden, Thaxted, Braintree, Great Dunmow and many others have risen and fallen, often leaving grand churches as memorials to their years of plenty, often derived from the fleece and the loom. Old trades have given way to new, and tourism has become the latest regional industry. More recent history will record the creation of towns like Basildon and Harlow, where the 20th century offered a modern solution to a contemporary problem.

Essex has never been able to ignore the proximity of London. In the 14th century the men of Essex were drawn to the capital in the Peasants' Revolt, and suffered for their presumption. Ilford and Romford were once villages with leafy lanes, but in time the city reached out and touched them, eventually obliging them to admit they were no longer part of Essex. Today's commuters struggle into the city by road and rail, from all parts of the county. But they cannot wait to return to their particular piece of rural England, for within a score of miles you will find industry and rolling farmland, suburbs and seclusion. There are parts of this county where there is such peace and perfection that the very existence of another, more boisterous, way of life seems to be in doubt.

Essex is still a farming county. Its pretty villages are set amid green fields, and the narrow roads are used by tractors and combines to the despair of impatient visitors. It continues to be a wealthy county, whatever the measure employed. It has managed to come to terms with its past and present. Two hundred years ago John Constable returned again and again to his favourite parts of Essex. His genius did so much to encapsulate not only the landscapes of Dedham Vale, but the very essence of English countryside at its best. Constable's Essex may still be seen and enjoyed, and for that we should be grateful and proud. Of course it has changed, but far more remarkable is the extent to which it has survived. Essex merits – and rewards – a much closer look.

Burnham on Crouch

It is perhaps astonishing that a small town on the banks of a fairly undistinguished river should be internationally renowned, yet Burnham on Crouch, known as 'the Pearl of the East Coast', hosts one of the major events of the yachting calendar, and has established itself as an exclusive sailing base and a mecca for all boating enthusiasts.

At one time Burnham was connected with oyster fishing, but the industry declined in the early part of the century, and although oysters and shellfish may still be bought locally it is no longer possible to breed oysters in the Crouch. Coincidentally, however, the 1900s saw the growing popularity of Burnham – at that time little more than a village – as a sailing centre, and nowadays most of the towns-people are in some way connected with boats. Two important Yacht Clubs are based here, the Royal Burnham and the Royal Corinthian. The latter moved to Burnham from its base in Kent in 1900; the present Clubhouse is one of the most striking buildings on the waterfront. Its gleaming white tiers won an award for the architect when they were first built in 1931, but they have always been somewhat controversial. A new marina has recently been established at the western end of the town, with high quality shipwright, engineering and rigging services for the yachtsman. It has the benefit of unrestricted access no matter what the state of the tide.

The town itself is approached by some difficult and winding roads, but there is a direct rail link with London, and Burnham's very position has to a certain extent preserved it from over development. It has cottages and shops in different styles and from different ages; but the High Street is particularly attractive in the informality of pink or yellow washed houses abutting white weatherboarding and mellow brick. This is one of the widest streets in Essex, and its main feature is a clock tower of 1877, recently restored. The Market Square has been the site of the Tuesday Market since the 14th century, and here oysters were sold and shipped in barrels to Holland. There are narrow streets leading southwards to the river, where it is pleasant to walk along the quay, past small boatyards and individual cottages with colourful gardens, and admire the broad vista of the Crouch. This river runs almost due east for 15 miles from Battles-bridge, the highest navigable point, to Shore Ends, and when the tide is low the mud flats can be described as dull; but to the visitor watching from the quayside at Burnham, nowhere could be more delightfully busy. This is particularly so during Burnham Week in August, when as many as 400 boats converge upon the town to compete in some 80 races, culminating in the prestigious Town Cup.

Thaxted

In every way Thaxted is a very fortunate town. It has a magnificent church, complete with soaring spire; it has a 15th century Guildhall which dominates the main street of the town, and it even has a splendid brick tower mill overlooking the fields which surround the town itself. Add to this a connection with two historical characters – one good and the other bad – and you have the perfect mix, well worth a visit.

The Guildhall was built by the Cutlers in the late 14th century, and the open ground floor would have housed the market. As the cutlery business declined the premises were used by the local council and by the Grammar School. It is now restored and open to visitors.

To the side of the Guildhall, in Stoney Lane, stands an antique shop which once provided brief employment for a butcher's boy called Dick Turpin. History remembers him for the various things he did after he was fired, but the link with Thaxted is real enough, for when the famous highwayman was arrested in York it was to this pretty Essex town that he sent for a character reference, and it was the failure of anyone to provide it that resulted in his execution in 1739.

The Church of St John the Baptist, St Mary and St Lawrence may appear to be a bit greedy for patronage, but it is big enough for them all, and richly deserves the special status. Step inside, and it becomes evident that its title of the finest parish church in the country is no idle boast, for the competition would have to be exceptional. The overwhelming impressions are of size, height and light. It is everything an English town church should be. The spire, which was 183 feet high, fell down and had to be rebuilt in 1822, and by mistake they made it two feet shorter, but it does not show!

Between the church and John Webb's Mill are two rows of pretty almshouses. The thatched one was originally the priest's dwelling, while the other building now houses three people.

All the roads of Thaxted are worth exploring, and the shops, houses and offices all represent sensible ways of using a varied historical legacy. Opposite the Church are the imposing facades of Clarance House, the King's Head and the Swan Hotel. The composer Gustav Holst wrote his most famous suite of music, 'The Planets', while living in a thatched cottage in Monk Street.

St Osyth's Priory

There can be few more tranquil spots than this. The village of St Osyth with its narrow streets and pretty weatherboarded houses stands somewhat isolated, cut off by marsh, creek, river and sea both to the east and to the south. Tucked away on the south eastern edge of the village stands the Priory, whose antiquity and beauty convey complete serenity. But it was not always so. The Priory was built on the remains of a nunnery founded by Osytha, the daughter of the first King of East Anglia. In her youth Osytha experienced a miraculous return to life after 3 days drowned; as a result, she renounced marriage to the King of Essex, and took the veil. She was given the village which now bears her name, and was Abbess here in AD 653 at the time of violent raids by the Danes upon the coast; she was tortured and eventually beheaded by these ruffians whose idolatry she steadfastly refused to accept. Where her body fell, a spring arose whose curative properties were afterwards proven; and the Saint, picking up her severed head, walked the quarter of a mile to the Church of St Peter and St Paul, where she knocked on the door with bloody hands.

Nowadays we have only this legend to remind us of the Saint, for her relics disappeared in the 16th century, and her statue, which stood between those of St Peter and St Paul in a niche of the great Gate House, was destroyed by the Puritans. Nevertheless, the legacy of this extraordinary figure is immense. The Priory is fronted by the magnificent Gate House, described as 'unexcelled by any monastic remains in the country'. The Gate House is of flint brick and stone and dates from about 1475. Passing through it, the visitor finds the lovely red brick buildings of later centuries, since the Abbey Church no longer survives, and the estate passed after the Dissolution to Lord D'Arcy, who made considerable additions. What we now see is a mixture of monastic remains (including the atmospheric Chapel, and the Abbot's Tower which affords a marvellous view over the Priory and beyond) and later buildings, one of which houses the Fitzwilliam Art Collection including paintings by Stubbs, Reynolds and Van Dyck. These buildings are set in a most beautiful and enormous deer park brightened by various gardens – the Water Garden with its lily pond, the Topiary Garden and the wonderful Rose Garden, all boasting an immaculate array of scented and colourful flowers.

Braintree & Bocking

These twin towns were amalgamated into an urban district in 1934, and they are both inextricably linked with weaving of silk and other textiles. They are particularly indebted to the Courtauld family whose company provided wealth for the town and whose benefactions still stand.

Bocking had for many years been the centre of a thriving industry producing baize, a coarse woollen cloth, and so the expertise of many generations of skilled workmen provided the Courtaulds with the foundations of their business. In the 17th century the Courtaulds had been Huguenot refugees fleeing persecution abroad; as the Napoleonic Wars cut off trade with the Continent, George Courtauld, great grandson of the original immigrant, had the foresight to change direction, and he went into silk throwing, with his first mill established in 1798 at Pebmarsh, to the north east of Halstead, then at Bocking (1816). By 1861 the mills were employing almost 3000 people. In 1854 Samuel had been wealthy enough to buy Gosfield Hall, much to the disgust of his aristocratic neighbours; shunned by them, he died a recluse. But the family continued to prosper, and the 1890s saw an expansion into man made fibres. In the early years of this century, the first silk rayon was produced at Halstead.

The Courtaulds' wealth led to the foundation of the Courtauld Institute of Art (1931), and was distributed through the town in numerous benefactions: the drinking fountain in the Market Square was erected in 1882 – it is now planted with flowers, but it is nevertheless a worthy centrepiece. The old Town Hall (1928) now houses a museum and an art gallery; there is a second fountain, showing a bronze of a boy with a fish, standing in front of St Michael's Church on the corner of the High Street. The Courtaulds also provided the clock in the tower. The hospital and the public gardens and recreation ground are similar creations by the Courtaulds.

Nowadays, the pedestrianised town centre draws shoppers from a wide area, and motorists are guided around a rather complicated one way system; but, despite the necessary interventions of the modern world, you may still see pretty cottages and more opulent houses belonging to the merchants' families, as well as some older inns. Especially notable is Bradford Street, one of the longest medieval streets in England, where Braintree and Bocking merge. Here and in Church Street lived the old weavers, who on fine days would sit outside their cottages and work, whilst indoors children would be winding the silk onto spools for the shuttles. A few of the old buildings are, alas, showing signs of neglect, but the old post mill in Church Street has been restored.

Clacton-on-Sea

The resorts of the Essex Sunshine Coast – Clacton, Holland-on-Sea, Frinton and Walton – were developed with the coming of the railway in the mid Victorian period, when they became accessible as day trip centres to weary city-dwellers. Now the name of Clacton-on-Sea is synonymous with the best sort of British holidays, characterised by deck chairs in the sun and a pier with all the fun of the fair.

At the end of the 1700s when doctors began to extol the benefits of sea-bathing, first Walton became popular, and then its neighbouring villages. The railway reached Clacton in 1882, and since then, generations of holiday makers have come to enjoy the resort. For Clacton has indeed a magnificent position in the county: south facing, with 7 miles of soft golden sand stretching in a gentle arc. At low tide the West Beach shelves gently into the water, and its cleanliness has earned the coveted blue flag. You can hire a deck chair and simply rest within earshot of the waves, or enjoy one of the beach activities, such as the sandcastle competitions. Or you can take a long walk along the promenade to the far south western end where you can buy fresh fish from the fishermen who have pulled their small boats up on to the sand. At this end of the beach, at Martello Bay (named after one of the three Martello Towers in the area) is a modern Watersports Centre. From here, the eye is irresistibly drawn to the pier, an enormous structure dating from 1866 and covering some 6.5 acres; it is renowned for its scores of attractions,

including a Living Ocean experience, Fourth Dimension space adventure and a roller skating rink. But there is much more to Clacton. Walk up the slope towards the town and you come to the most beautiful seafront gardens, lovingly tended and delighting the eye with their many colours. Here is the most perfect place to sit and soak up the atmosphere with the sunshine. Overlooking the gardens and Marine Parade are elegant hotels and boarding houses, behind which lie a modern shopping centre and yet more amusements for young and old, including the Leisure Centre and Magic City, a futuristic playground for children. In short, Clacton is a resort which offers entertainment of all kinds, but where you can also relax and feel at home.

Dedham

Dedham Vale – the very name is evocative, bringing to mind the countryside idyll as shown in the paintings of John Constable. This border land between Suffolk and Essex has not radically changed since those times, and attracts many visitors who often choose to stroll along the River Stour between Flatford Mill and Dedham, whose church spire was a favourite of Constable's, and which he represented in many of his landscapes.

Dedham is undoubtedly pretty and well aware of it. The traffic on the main A12 speeds away at a distance of a couple of miles, and the lanes leading to Dedham provide a complete contrast – tree-lined, lazy and familiar. We cross the river – the boundary between the two counties – and at once see a water mill, a Victorian replacement of the one owned by Golding Constable. The town has a single main street running parallel with the river; it is leafy and picturesque. There are many ancient buildings, some of them with later facades, but blending together in a very satisfactory way. The most impressive is the towering Church of St Mary the Virgin, built at the time of the town's greatest prosperity which grew from the cloth trade. Completed in 1520 after only 30 years work, the church has a harmony which imparts itself to the rest of the village. Here in the main street old inns such as the Sun and the Marlborough Head show timbers and colour wash; there are plenty of Georgian houses, too. Sherman's, opposite the church, is apparently one such, but a closer look shows the brick facade, with its pilasters and sundial, to be a later addition to a very old building. It once belonged to the forebears of General Sherman, the great American Civil War leader, and is now in the care of the National Trust. To the east of the Church is a sort of town square, with a stone cross, and nearby is the old Grammar School. This is the school attended by John Constable, who found its masters more tolerant of his artistic leanings than those of his former school at Lavenham, where he had been most unhappy. Further east is the Art & Craft Centre, situated in the old Congregational Chapel. As well as a Toy Museum, there are displays of painting, pottery and traditional handicrafts, for which the area is now well known.

A second artist associated with Dedham is Sir Alfred Munnings, whose home, Castle House, is situated about a mile to the south east. His studio has been kept as it was in his lifetime, and during the summer the public may see many of his paintings here.

Harwich & Parkeston Quay

From Parkeston Quay as many as 2 million passengers are carried each year to Scandinavia, Holland and Germany; so for many, Harwich has become the Gateway to the Continent. This association with the sea spans the centuries. Harwich enjoys a prime geographical position, set on the southern side of the broad and deep stretch of water formed by the estuaries of the Orwell and the Stour. In 1661 mail packets began to sail from here to Holland and when the franchise for this was lost to the faster steamboats from Kent in 1836, the men of Harwich turned their attention to passenger services. Ferry services to Rotterdam were inaugurated in 1863, and the Railway Hotel (now the Town Hall) was built on the Quay to accommodate passengers. When this proved to be too small an area, marshes were reclaimed upstream and Parkeston Quay was opened.

Harwich is perhaps best seen from the water;

viewed from the north, the town lies on the estuary like an old Flemish painting, with the spire of St Nicholas's Church crowning the horizon. But the brightly-coloured buoys of the Trinity House Buoy Yard bring us up to date, and remind us that Harwich fulfils an important role in the modern shipping world: it is the largest of the Trinity House depots, controlling an area from Berwick-upon-Tweed in the north to Lyme Bay in the south west; and the old-fashioned appearance of the town belies the fact that it is still the place for pilot cutters and a lifeboat, and that the radar operations room controls all the shipping in this extensive estuary.

The narrow streets of Old Harwich date from early medieval times, and we can begin to appreciate the fascinating historical associations: Drake, Hawkins and Frobisher sailed from here on various expeditions against the Spanish, and Elizabeth I described the town as 'a pretty place and lacks nothing'; in King's Head Street, close to the Quay, there is a house once owned by Christopher Jones, master of the 'Mayflower'. Later the diarist Samuel Pepys was MP for Harwich at a time when it was the HQ for the King's Navy. Other historic buildings and monuments include the High and Low Lighthouses, built in 1818 to guide sailors safely through the sandbanks offshore by lining up their two lights. They have since been made redundant, firstly because the excavation of clay from Beacon Cliff caused a shift in the course of the channels, and secondly because of automation. The Low Lighthouse is now the town's maritime museum.

Hadleigh Castle

In one sense people have always come to this site for the view. It offers a spectacular vantage point over the River Thames, and in times gone past this has required some form of military control, for it commands the approaches to London.

The temptation to assume that the ruins result from desperate battles of the past must be resisted, as they are simply the result of land subsidence or the fact that over the centuries they have been plundered as a sort of second-hand quarry. But back in 1231 the builders found this an ideal site for a fortification, and working to the instructions of Hubert de Burgh, Chief Justiciar to King Henry III they created a powerful and impressive oasis of stability in an area likely to be threatened from the sea, particularly from France. Unfortunately for Hubert he fell from favour only a year after the work began, and Hadleigh Castle was completed by Edward III, who used it both as a prison and as a Royal residence – although different people were involved! It is hard to picture the scene today, since for much of the time the chief attraction of the castle to its royal owners was as a hunting residence.

Over several centuries it was the custom for kings to make a gift of the castle to their queens, although what use they made of it can only be imagined. Henry VIII gave this castle in turn to three of his six wives. In the 16th century, during the reign of Edward VI it was sold to Lord Rich (of Felsted) for £700, and he plundered it for the stone which he used in his other projects in the county.

Today the castle ruins provide a superb reason for climbing up to the site, and the views across to Canvey Island and out over the Thames to Kent repay the effort. Canvey Island is created from river silt, and it was only in the 17th century that Dutch engineers, notably Vermuyden, encircled it with a protective wall and made possible the building of permanent structures such as we see today. Of course the oil refinery and natural gas tanks are evidence of its industrial importance, but the island has a less severe aspect at the eastern end, where there are areas of farmland and for leisure. As in the Dengie Marshes, local men had difficulty in keeping a wife in the damp and unhealthy conditions, and many were widowers over and over again: Daniel Defoe writes of an Islander who had just wedded his 25th wife, while his son had already married 14 times!

A Country Park was created around Hadleigh Castle in 1987, and the visitor can enjoy signposted paths which take in woodland, ponds and grasslands, with a profusion of birds, insects and butterflies.

John Constable visited Hadleigh Castle in 1814, and made a number of sketches. At the time he wrote to his wife, Maria: 'At Hadleigh there is a ruin of a castle which from its situation is a really fine place – it commands a view of the Kent hills, the Nore and North Foreland and looking many miles to sea.' Fifteen years later the sketches became the basis of one of his last oil paintings.

Great Dunmow

'Dunmow probably has more tradition than any other town in Essex, and is known wherever the English language is understood, for here in Dunmow is the home of the Flitch itself'. These words of a senior Essex archivist sum up the attractions of Great Dunmow; for if this market town is no longer as important as it once was, it retains much of its ancient heritage and traditions. Every leap year a side of bacon (or 'flitch') is still presented to the couple claiming to have been harmoniously married for a year and a day. The custom dates back as far as 1120, and was originally accredited to the monks of the Priory of Little Dunmow, some three miles away.

The custom was continued even after the Dissolution, and its fame was widespread. One year, 5000 spectators blocked the roads for miles around in an attempt to view the couple, who capitalised on their success by selling off slices of the Flitch. The custom lapsed in the mid 18th century but in 1855 it was revived – in Great Dunmow, since the Lord of the Manor refused permission for it to occur in Little Dunmow – and is still a notable local event, celebrated with a pageant or fair.

Great Dunmow has ancient origins. It was the hill fort of a Celtic tribe, and later a Roman garrison town on Stane Street, the old way joining St Albans and Colchester. In medieval times the influx of Flemish weavers brought the skills of weaving 'bays and says', thick woollen cloth, and when in the 16th century hops were first grown in the town, brewing became another local industry. Dunmow was granted charters by Mary and Elizabeth, and many of the notable buildings date from this era. The High Street (formerly Stane Street) has a number of old inns and merchants' houses; the Saracen's Head, a fine posting house, stands opposite the old Town Hall, amongst a group of Elizabethan buildings in Market Street. Nearby is the Chestnuts, the house of a Dr Raynor who kept his leeches in 'the Doctor's Pond' off North Street; here, too, Lionel Lukin tested the first self-righting life boat in 1785. At the end of the Causeway is the brick and plaster Clock House – the unusual one-handed clock is in the turret – home to St Anne Line, one of the martyrs of Dunmow, who was hanged at Tyburn in 1601 for sheltering Jesuit priests. These are just some of the buildings of interest; there are many more.

Nowadays Great Dunmow has been bypassed by the busy main road, and it is easy to see how it can be said to lie at the heart of rural Essex, surrounded by little villages – the Rodings, the Easters, the Willingales – and the green downs and commons bordering the quiet River Chelmer, held in trust for the townspeople by the Parish Council; but on Tuesdays when the market is held, you can still enjoy the bustle of this old market town.

Colchester

Britain's oldest recorded town is entitled to boast of its Roman past because it is so tangible. Colchester was once ruled over by Old King Cole of nursery-rhyme fame, and when the Roman legions invaded Britain it had become the tribal capital of the Catuvellauni, the most powerful and sophisticated inhabitants on the island. Cunobelinus was their leader; we know him better, perhaps, as Shakespeare's Cymbeline. It was the death of this man which caused the Romans to mount their successful invasion in AD 43 and their moment of triumph was the capture of Colchester by the Emperor Claudius. When Boudicca attacked and destroyed Colchester, her army massacred the Roman population in the temple, which had been built in honour of Claudius. Later, of course, she was defeated, and Colchester was rebuilt with impressive defences. Even to this day a fine Roman wall surrounds the city centre.

In medieval times the Normans used the site of the temple for the foundations of their castle, built within ten years of the Conquest. The visitor has the unusual experience of being able to pass from Norman to Roman simply by descending to the cellars! Originally Colchester castle had four storeys, but even with just two it is impressive, and provides an excellent home for the fascinating museum collection. In 1218 the French captured the castle for a brief period, after which it became a prison. One unfortunate was tortured by the thumbscrews in 1406 'till the blood oozed forth.'

Tudor Colchester saw the arrival of the Flemish weavers, whose skill ensured prosperity and employment for the town. During the Civil War there was excitement when Roundhead forces besieged the Royalists, and executed the officers in the castle grounds. 'The Siege House', a timber building at the bottom of East Street, still proudly displays the shot holes.

There can be few towns which have managed so successfully to combine their history with the modern needs of a busy, attractive shopping centre. The Roman remains share public car parks, and the pretty open spaces and brightly lit shopping precincts stand on the ashes of Boudicca's victims! Even the military connection continues, with army barracks and training areas on the outskirts, and a splendid military tattoo in the castle grounds. The annual Oyster Feast in October is a reminder that the River Colne has played an important part in the town's history, and that tradition is still highly regarded and enjoyed.

Brightlingsea

Brightlingsea has been inhabited ever since the Romans lived at Camulodunum, modern-day Colchester, some six miles upstream. Oysters were cultivated then, as the disused oyster pits near the Town Hard prove. But Brightlingsea's continuous history really dates from Saxon times. In Old English, the village was 'Brightling's eg' or 'eye', (meaning 'island'), and any map shows how the arms of Flag Creek to the east and Alresford Creek to the north meet in marshy land to cut off Brightlingsea from the rest of the county.

The town has the distinction of being the only one of the Cinque Ports outside Kent and Sussex, and even today, town officials have to swear an oath of allegiance to the Mayor of Sandwich. There is no doubt that the history of Brightlingsea, and its continued existence, owes everything to the sea. It was for many centuries an important boat building centre and supplied ships to the King and the Royal Navy as early as the days of Edward III; it was a trading post, exporting cloth to the Netherlands and importing wine; the men of Brightlingsea were fishermen, for oysters (as far afield as Holland) and for sprats, whilst their wives and children combed the shore for nuggets of copperas, which was used in the dyeing industry. Early this century, Brightlingsea built ocean racers which Victorian gentlemen sailed in the summer, with local men as crew. This inextricable link with the sea, caused by the safe haven of Brightlingsea creek, still continues: Brightlingsea is a centre par excellence for the yachting fraternity, and provides many other marine activities besides, including waterskiing and power boats. A new steel piled wharf allows coasters to unload coal and aggregate and load grain – so that the life of Brightlingsea continues unabated.

There are some notable buildings to attest to this success. The 13th century Church of All Saints is situated on the higher ground beyond the town, and confirms the strong links with the sea. Its grandeur was derived from the endowments of wealthy merchants whose names can be read on the memorial brasses. The 97 feet high tower was used as a navigational aid until recent times (it may be seen to a distance of 17 miles to sea). A Victorian minister, Canon Pertwee, used to climb the tower in stormy weather and place a lamp there to aid homecoming sailors. It was his idea, too, to begin the decorative frieze which runs round the inside of the Church and which commemorates all those men of Brightlingsea who have perished in the deep. Another eminent building is Jacobes Hall, the 13th century former Moot Hall; timber framed, it has an undulating tiled roof and an exterior staircase, and is thought to be the oldest building in continuous occupation in the county.

Waltham Abbey

There is a story that Tovi the Dane, Standard Bearer to King Harold, discovered a stone crucifix, and began a search for the right place to found a church to display it. One day, during his travels, the oxen refused to move, and Tovi had found God's choice; the Church of the Holy Cross, and St Lawrence, which was to become Waltham Abbey.

King Harold worshipped at Holy Cross, and apparently was cured of a sickness. Miracles were reported, and the place became a pilgrim centre. As he came south with his army in 1066, Harold paused at Waltham to pray and rest, but this did not prevent his death and defeat at Hastings. Eventually his body was brought back to this church, and today a stone marks the last resting place of this famous warrior.

The Norman Abbey dates from the 12th century, and was built by Henry II as part of his penance for precipitating Becket's death. It was

built in prestigious Caen stone. Only the nave survives today, but the enormous columns with their grooved zig zag patterns indicate the magnificence of the original concept. Harold's tomb had been before the High Altar, but changes at this time resulted in his tomb being left outside! It is difficult to appreciate how completely the vast abbey dominated the town. The brick Gatehouse and Harold's Bridge date from the 14th century and suggest how wealthy and impressive it was.

Thomas Tallis, described as 'the father of English cathedral music' was organist at Waltham Abbey for its last two years of Roman Catholic worship, and wrote one of his most complex motets for the choir. About two thirds of the Abbey failed to survive the Reformation in the 16th century, but the need for a parish church saved the nave, and maybe Henry VIII's fondness for the place helped as well. In 1552 the Tower collapsed, and although it was rebuilt, the bells had to be recast; now they provide one of the finest peals in England. The interior is an interesting mixture of styles and dates, but they exist together remarkably well, and the Norman features are complemented by a 19th century Rose Window and a reredos showing scenes from the early life of Christ. There is a museum in the undercroft which is exceptionally well presented.

The grounds are now a public park, and in early summer the rose garden is exquisite. The River Lea flows close to the Abbey Church and the well kept lawns make an ideal spot for a picnic.

Harlow

If an architect designs a town, and then decides to live the rest of his life in it, there can be no question of a lack of confidence. So it was with Sir Frederick Gibberd, who in 1947 became the planner of Harlow, and found himself responsible for creating a city which would cover 6,500 acres where before there had been only scattered villages. He saw his ideas come to fruition as the population rose to 70,000 and the skyline was broken by imaginative shapes in concrete and glass. He died in Harlow in 1984 and, like Christopher Wren, his monument is all around us.

Harlow tackled the problems of modern city life in a bold, imaginative way. It was the pioneer of pedestrian centres, and today's shoppers still enjoy the paved courtyards which make shopping safer and more enjoyable. Landscaped gardens are never far away, and in them lakes and fountains provide sound and movement, while sculptures by the very best of modern artists are at almost every corner. Cycle trackways were another innovation which is now accepted as standard.

In the 1950s it was referred to as Pram City, because its birth rate was so much higher than the national average! Today, these young people have the very best amenities within easy reach. When it was opened in 1960 here was Britain's first 'Sportcentre', and it continues to grow, with a modern ski slope being among the latest attractions. The River Stort, which forms the Essex County line at this point, offers boating and other gentler pastimes. Parndon Wood Nature Reserve comprises two trails, and a comprehensive exhibition centre.

But there were people living in this area long before the developments of this century, and several interesting museums chronicle the story. The Harlow Study Centre is located in a 13th century church, and beside it stands the Monks Tithe Barn which is a Visitors' Centre. Passmore's Museum is in a Georgian house, and tells the story of the city from Roman times. More modern is the Mark Hall Cycle Museum, opened in 1982, and occupying the former stables of the Hall. Queen Elizabeth I is reputed to have stayed, not once, but thrice in the Hall, but it has not survived.

The Harvey Centre, with its two-storey, modern design shopping pavilion even offers a climatically controlled central mall. In such surroundings, where nature is afforded every consideration, it was an appropriate decision to name the pubs after moths and butterflies! Time has been kind to Harlow. It has weathered well, and come of age.

Maldon & Heybridge

The writer Arnold Bennet was a great fan of the River Blackwater, describing it as a noble stream. Others have echoed his verdict. No place is more agreeable for the visitor; it has a pretty collection of sailing boats, riverside walks and attractive pubs. But once these two towns were the centre of a bitter struggle for supremacy.

Maldon in the 18th century had a stranglehold on the river trade to Chelmsford, and grew wealthy on the tolls it collected. Alternative routes were considered and rejected – or outwitted – for over a hundred years, until 1798 which saw the opening of the 14 mile long Heybridge and Chelmer and Blackwater Navigation Canal. This leaves the River Blackwater at the stretch known as Collier's Reach, where the flat, undisturbed vastness of the bird reserve of Northey Island forms the opposite bank.

One of the most famous views of Maldon is from the riverside walk, looking back over the Marine Lake to the white steeple of St Mary's Church – known as 'The Mariners' Beacon' since its addition to the 12th century church in 1740. The lake is ideal for children, with its little sandy shore; boats are pulled up all along the river's edge on one side, and on the other, the ground rises to the green lawns and colourful flowerbeds of the extensive Promenade Park and Recreation Grounds. A little further upstream on Hythe Quay are to be found the spectacular Thames sailing barges, with their rust brown sails and shining woodwork. At the turn of the century, these numbered 2000; they transported stacks of hay – hence their nickname, 'stackies' – piled high on the wide deck, for the horses of the London markets and would return with manure and straw; now there are often less than a dozen, some available for charter. In June is held the Blackwater Barge Match, and there are other important races held here. There is also a new purification plant for oysters which are bred in Goldhanger Creek. The other major product for which Maldon is famous is its sea salt; the river water is especially briny as it can evaporate in the drying easterly wind on the wide mudflats and saltings; from the last century the process has taken place in huge vats housed in black tarred sheds by the water's edge.

The town itself is full of historical interest – it is one of the oldest recorded towns in Essex, and already had a thousand inhabitants at the time of the Domesday survey.

Layer Marney

Henry, Lord Marney was Captain of the King's Guard to Henry VIII. His family had lived at Layer Marney, near Colchester, since the time of William the Conqueror and he wanted to proclaim his wealth and importance in that most Tudor of ways – building. He chose to create a great residence, beginning with a gatehouse of unprecedented splendour. His death in 1523 did not affect the work, but when his only son died just two years later the family ceased to exist, and today only the gatehouse stands to suggest the grandeur of the Marney dream.

Although gatehouses originally had a military purpose the arrival of gunpowder did not render them entirely redundant for they were transformed into symbols of status and ambition. Layer Marney Tower stands over 80 feet high, and is constructed of brick and Italian terracotta, which was very advanced for England at that time. The inner turrets have eight windows, one above the other, while the outer turrets make do with seven. The windows are ornate and regular, confirming that they were not meant to withstand a siege. The view from the roof is well worth the climb, especially as the rooms on the way include displays of the Tower's history, which repay careful reading for they are outstandingly thorough.

The gardens are beautifully maintained, and the view of the Tower from the end of the gravel drive is impressive. Near the Tower is a splendid Tudor hall, which began life as the stables and grooms' house. Now it has been perfectly restored and is used for receptions, parties and even Tudor banquets. The sense of polished timber is truly exquisite and it must provide an unforgettable memory for wedding couples.

Just as close to the Tower is the Church of St Mary the Virgin, built by the Marney family in about 1500. Three monuments of full length armoured knights depict the Marney family. William died in 1414 and his effigy is made of alabaster, but appropriately grand is the black marble figure under a terracotta canopy, for this is Henry, Lord Marney, the greatest of the line. His son, John, completes the trio of illustrious magnates.

The present owners are Nicholas and Sheila Charrington whose family bought the property in 1958. They have introduced a rare breeds park, specialising in animals likely to have been on the estate at the time of the Marneys. These include Dexters and Red Poll cattle, Norfolk longhorn and Soay sheep, Golden Guernsey goats and British Saddleback pigs. A deer park is another reminder of Layer Marney's golden age.

Saffron Walden

This picturesque market town stands at the north western corner of the county, surrounded by beautiful rolling countryside. Originally there was a Saxon settlement here ('Waledana', meaning the valley of the Britons, was the basis for its name), but the town grew and prospered as a result of the cloth trade, and for four centuries had a second important export: the stamens or 'chives' of the saffron crocus which was cultivated in its millions here and which was prized until the end of the 18th century as a dyestuff, in cooking and in medicine. It is this tiny flower which gave the town its distinctive name and its symbol, to be found carved around the Church and in the town's coat of arms.

After the Norman Conquest, the lands were given to the powerful baron, Geoffrey de Mandeville, and he built a castle on the high ground overlooking the valley of the River Cam. The place had strategic importance as the gateway into this part of Essex; but the castle was largely destroyed within a century by Henry II who sought to suppress the power of such barons. Now only some of the massive flint walls of the keep survive. Within the castle grounds is the local museum; and the Castle Green, now known as the Common, is a wide open space, at the far end of which is the famous Turf Maze.

The town is crowned by the Church of St Mary the Virgin, whose 193 feet high tower and spire dominate the town. The church, originally Norman, was extensively remodelled during the town's wealthiest days in the 15th and 16th centuries, and it is one of the largest and most beautiful churches in the county. Light and airy, it contains many interesting memorials, including the tomb of Lord Chancellor Thomas Audley who was the builder of the first great mansion at nearby Audley End.

As for the rest of the town, the ancient mixes happily with the more modern. The 14th century buildings include the former Sun Inn in Castle Street where the outer walls are decorated with 17th century pargeting (raised plasterwork); you can clearly see the hero Tom Hickathrift fighting a giant armed with only a wagon wheel and an axle. Other buildings of note include old inns such as the Eight Bells in Bridge Street and the Cross Keys at the bottom of the High Street. The Youth Hostel, at the junction of Castle Street and Bridge Street, is probably the finest medieval building in the town. Wherever you look, there are carved beams, overhanging gables and crooked walls washed in pink, white and green, and all add to the charming effect.

Around the Market Place stand buildings dating from Georgian and Victorian times. Close by, however, the narrow Rows bear names which witness to the town's older past, when market traders' stalls were replaced by permanent shops as trade expanded: Butchers' Row, Mercers' Row, Fish Row and Pig Street give a fine flavour of how the town used to be.

Tollesbury Lofts

There was a time when Tollesbury was a fishing village with about 100 boats moored there, all involved in the business of catching sprats for London. But the arrival of the railway meant wealthy sportsmen moored their yachts on the Blackwater, and left them there to be cared for when the season was over. As many as forty boats provided quite a lot of employment for the local river folk. The fishermen were much in demand for their services as crewmen on the yachts of the wealthy, and so in winter they laboured to pull in ropes attached to nets, while in summer they struggled to gain control of yet more ropes, this time attached to jib sails and such like.

The heyday for this dual employment was the turn of the century, and from this busy time date the distinctive sail lofts, which stand at the water's edge by Woodrolfe Creek. They were used to dry out sails, and contain racks and pulleys for this purpose. Their clapboard planks may once have been stained dark, or as at present, painted, but it is remarkable how they have continued to house the trades which depend on seafarers. They stand on stone plinths to protect them from the rising tide.

Today Tollesbury maintains its association with the yachting fraternity, and in the saltings and creeks there are scores of sailing craft, new and old, and from dawn to dusk there is the agreeable prospect for walkers of being able to watch people at work! It is a timeless stretch of the river, and in the evening, whatever the state of the tide, it is easy to imagine the appeal this place had held for marin-ers and boat builders. One of the international yachts berthed here in the years before the First World War was the 80ft 'Merrymaid', and it is still at anchor on the site of its triumphs.

The Church of St Mary provides evidence of the heyday of Tollesbury with its Seafarers' Window. From this village many yachtsmen planned their tactics for the great races, including the America's Cup. The window was donated by an American banker, Frederick Hasler, who took part in international races. It shows among other things a 'billy boy' (a clinker built coaster), and a barge, a 'stackie' – which is a barge stacked high with hay bales, and the familiar oyster smack.

Chelmsford

Chelmsford is situated at the confluence of the Rivers Can and Chelmer, and has had a strategic importance since Roman times. It has been identified as Caesaromagus (the Plain of Caesar), and as such was one of the three marching camps on the route from London to the capital of East Anglia at Colchester. It was possessed of temples, baths, theatres and a market place.

There are some impressive buildings today too, for example the Shire Hall (1789–91) which stands in Tindal Square at the heart of the town. This was built by John Johnson, the County Surveyor, and there was a Corn Exchange in the basement. Close by, and a haven of tranquillity in the bustle of the town centre, is the Cathedral – one of the smallest in England, since it was formerly a simple parish church. It dates largely from the 15th century, although some traces of Roman stonework have been found. It has undergone many changes in its long life: in 1800, workmen digging a new grave in

the aisle weakened the pillars and caused most of the church to collapse, necessitating a full programme of rebuilding and embellishment. In 1914, the church was elevated to the status of a cathedral in line with the creation of the diocese of Chelmsford – one of the most populous in the country, with over 2 million people – and was subsequently enlarged. The South Porch (about 1460) was restored in 1953 by the Essex Friends of the American People as a memorial to the men of the United States Air Force who were stationed in Essex. In 1983 further improvements were made, including the moving of the side chapels (dedicated to St Cedd and St Peter), and the refurbishment of the interior, so that the whole has a more modern appearance and can be used for dramatic and musical functions: the Cathedral Festival, held annually in May, has in a very short time established itself as a prestigious event, attracting musicians, artists and street theatre players from all over the country.

From the time of the Reformation, most of the town was owned by a single family, the Mildmays, and in 1591 a survey reported that Chelmsford had some 300 habitations, 'divers of them seemly for gentlemen'. The 14 mile long Chelmer and Blackwater Navigation linked the town with the Heybridge Basin, and enabled the swift and cheap importing of timber. This aided the development of the town; but it was the coming of the railway which prompted the selling of some of the Mildmay estates and the subsequent residential and industrial developments.

Audley End

The first view of Audley End is impressive. It stands at the centre of a lush panorama formed by a cricket field, a gentle river and a vast lawn. An enormous building composed of warm coloured stone, intricate windows, grand porches and all surmounted by copper turret caps, rises perfectly out of the landscape to complete the view. As with so many great historic houses the effect is entirely deliberate, for the visitor is meant to be taken aback by its splendour. But the real surprise is that what we see today is only about half the original!

Thomas Howard, Earl of Suffolk, was Lord Treasurer to James I. He began building Audley End in 1605, and from the first it was meant to be a palace. The obvious comparison is with Hampton Court, and perhaps he would have done well to pursue the analogy, for in the same way as Wolsey lost his palace at Hampton because it rivalled the power of his king, Howard upset James I who accused him of using money from the Royal funds, and briefly sent him to prison. The worst part of the punishment was to follow. Denied his lucrative government post, Howard had to return to Audley End, and attempt to pay for the work he had in hand. Of course, he found it impossible, a sentiment his successors shared over the centuries. For a time it was the property of several 17th century kings, but as none of them paid the Suffolk family for it, the property was returned in 1701.

Throughout the 18th century a combination of renovation and demolition produced the building we enjoy today. The superb Great Hall exemplifies this process, for it rightly belongs to the original scheme, although the great oak screen, fireplace and staircase have all been altered for better or worse. One family member observed: 'For the open screen of stone we are indebted to the bad taste of Sir John Vanbrugh.' Every room in the house contains treasures and curiosities which reflect its varied fortunes.

The gardens and grounds are the work of those two indefatigable innovators of 18th century taste, Robert Adam and 'Capability' Brown. The former is responsible among other things for the delightfully named Tea House Bridge, and the latter provided the house and its guests with parklands to look good in. Today the thousands of visitors have a rich choice before them, for in addition to the pleasures of inspecting the house and its ample grounds, they can watch cricket, learn about falconry, thrill to re-enactments of civil war battles and even weep into the night watching old movies in the open air.

Queen Elizabeth II Bridge, Dartford

This magnificent bridge over the River Thames was opened by HM The Queen on October 30th 1991, and answered a prayer from motorists who had endured the traffic jams of the M25 only to discover that queues for the tunnel were even worse. Today, the traveller uses the bridge to pass from Essex to Kent, and the tunnel to return. All the toll booths are on the southern end so Essex is entitled to reject any bad feeling the charges may occasion!

Like all great engineering feats, bridges appeal to our sense of beauty, too, and the Dartford Bridge is no exception. It crosses London's mighty river with such simple grace that the four lanes of fast traffic pass between four giant pylons and arrive on the other side almost effortlessly. But statistics reveal the true nature of the achievement.

This is a cable-stayed design, with a total length of 2,872 metres, making it the second longest of its kind in the world. The roadway is 65 metres above the river, and the pylons are 84 metres high. The central span is 450 metres long. There are a total of 112 cables, weighing on average 15 tonnes each, giving a grand total of 1,600 tonnes. More useless (to the layman) but interesting information: the bridge used 750,000 high strength bolts, and requires 48,800 gallons of paint to keep it in trim! The bridge and tunnel are expected to cope with up to 135,000 vehicles per day, and to have a life of 120 years.

Close by is the recent shopping phenomenon – Thurrock Lakeside. Attractively built beside the 20 acre Alexandra Lake, this complex of large stores (including all the great High Street names), restaurants, boutiques, cinema and play areas is among the largest in Europe. The crowds come from far afield, and not just from the London region, making use of the 9,000 car park spaces! From the outside the influence of the Crystal Palace is immediately evident. Inside, the theme continues as bright light pours through acres of glass, and shopping malls thrive in a tubular framework connected by gentle escalators, which rise from a ground floor where greenery surrounds attractive pools and fountains. The effect is enticing and relaxing. This is a place for more than mere shopping – it is a day out in a retail theme park.

Finchingfield

The village of Finchingfield may be small, but the view across the pond to pretty white painted cottages rising gently towards the church of St John the Baptist, is surely familiar to most of us; and justly so, since this contains all the quintessential elements of the perfect English scene. The village rewards the visitor who takes the time to walk around and take a closer look at the features which make it so photogenic.

This part of Essex is full of picturesque vistas, but this is probably the finest of them all. Here a tributary of the River Pant widens to make a duck pond crossed by a narrow red brick bridge. On either side are stretches of green, with the four roads leading up and out of the village. The cottages and inns are often very old. Some are Georgian fronted, others have barge board or whitewashed plasterwork, but they please with their variety and neatness. Up the hill, you will see the Guildhall and Almshouses (c.1500), which once housed the village school and now have a museum; pass through the archway to one side and you find yourself in the churchyard, looking up at the tower. The leaded spire which once crowned the tower was blown down in a storm and replaced with the unusual white cupola which still houses the Angelus bell. The lower levels of the tower are Norman, but the principal building of the Church took place in the 14th century. Inside, the two chapels each has an interesting story. On the south side is the Berners Chapel, which has a marvellous tomb chest surmounted by a brass, and dating from 1523. On the shoulders of Sir John Berners may be seen the figure of his pet monkey, which earned his undying gratitude when with its screeches it alerted his son to a fire which subsequently destroyed the house. The North Chapel is the Kempe Chapel, with memorials to the family who in Elizabethan times built nearby Spains Hall. William Kempe in 1621 wrongly accused his wife of infidelity. When he discovered his mistake, he vowed himself to silence, and although his wife died in 1623, he 'did hold his peace for seaven yeares'. In 1628, weakened and ailing, William found he had entirely lost the power of speech and could no longer utter a cry for help; and so he died. Spains Hall, about half a mile away, has magnificent gardens which are well worth a visit. The Hall is approached through that part of the village known as Duck End. Here you will see the 18th century Post Mill – one of eight which once graced the parish – now acquired for the village by the County Council, and with its fine white sails restored. It fittingly completes the idyllic scene.

Hedingham Castle

The De Vere family came over with William the Conqueror, fought for him at Hastings, and Hedingham was one of their rewards. In 1140 Aubrey De Vere, Chamberlain to King Stephen, began to build the present castle. The architect – or ingeniator – was the Archbishop of Canterbury, who must have been a man of wide talents! There is some evidence that he designed both Hedingham and Rochester castles because they are similar. As it stands today it is a near perfect Norman Keep, 100 feet high, and surrounded by grassland where once the inner bailey defences stood.

The walls are 12 feet thick at the base, and the ashlar stone, which came from Barnack in Northampton, was a piece of extravagance not lost on De Vere's neighbours. Some of the scaffolding holes may still be seen. The stairway to the castle is meant to be awkward, for this enhanced its defensive capabilities, offering any attacker a narrow approach, ending with a right angle and a stout oak door. The Norman chevrons are still clear, as are the grooves for the portcullis. Even supposing an entrance was forced the spiral stairway from the Garrison Room comprises 124 steps, and because the spiral ascends in a clockwise direction the right handed defenders would have the advantage all the way up.

The Garrison floor was where the rank and file soldiers spent their lives, but above them, the Banqueting Hall was for the owners, and it had a fireplace and would have been relatively comfortable. The main arch is 28 feet across, making it the largest Norman arch anywhere. Here would take place the entertainments and feasts so beloved of film makers and novelists! The gallery for this floor is actually tunnelled through the great stone walls. The Lord and his family had some privacy in their apartments on the Dormitory floor above, but in times of trouble the castle could not permit such luxuries, and soldiers would have been everywhere.

The De Vere family played quite an important part in English history, and this was where they lived, hunted, entertained and used their influence. John De Vere, 13th Earl of Oxford, was a staunch supporter of Henry VII, and entertained his sovereign at Hedingham, expecting only compliments. The King had noticed, however, that De Vere had more retainers than the law allowed, and so even though they had made the visit exceptionally agreeable, the noble offender was fined very heavily, and forced into debt as a result.

The 17th Earl obtained degrees at Oxford and Cambridge before he was 16, and served as both soldier and sailor in the Spanish wars, while finding the time to travel extensively throughout Europe. He served Queen Elizabeth and was a glittering member of her legendary court. It is this gentleman who is thought by some to be the true author of the works commonly ascribed to William Shakespeare. Many famous writers have advanced his claims, offering strong evidence in his favour, but the mystery will probably never be resolved.

Mersea Island

A channel called the Pyefleet separates Mersea Island from the mainland, and it is crossed by a road bridge, with the unhelpful name of The Strood. This means marshy land and so really refers to the ground either side. When the tide is exceptionally high, the bridge is under water so the island status is well deserved, and the character of Mersea is distinctive and keenly protected.

The Romans are said to have established a military base here, and there is the possibility that there was a lighthouse too. Beneath the Church of St Peter and St Paul the remains of a Roman villa were discovered, while to the west of the church there is evidence of an important grave to a wealthy Briton, who nevertheless chose to be buried in the Roman manner. But the most important contribution from this period is 'ostrea edilis' – the common British oyster, also known as West Mersea Natives.

Oysters have always played a key role in the economy of the island, and the old oyster beds can still be seen at the water's edge in West Mersea, with their worn and weed-draped timbers probably little changed down the centuries. Today, the harvest of the river is kept in tanks which are housed in sheds to avoid such calamities as the winter of 1962–63 when the sea froze and the oysters were devastated.

Although the island has only a total of 8 square miles, there is a considerable difference between East and West. The former is more rural, and includes Cudmore Grove, a 35 acre Country Park, with picnic area and beach, and the usual amenities for the holiday maker. West Mersea is more of a town – indeed the name for the furthest corner is The City – and here the occupations are more noticeably concerned with the shore line, such as boat-building, yachting and of course oyster fishing.

Throughout the day and well into the evening the water's edge is a place of constant activity, whether it be boat repairs, sailing preparation or visitors enjoying the sights and sounds. The cottages here are delightful, many of them weatherboarded, and set in pretty gardens. Some of the residents remain afloat to a certain extent for there are quite a lot of houseboats in varying degrees of seaworthiness!

In times past smuggling was one of the main pursuits of the islanders, and they were canny enough, or sufficiently generous, to keep the Revenue Men at a distance, for it was said that every pub on Mersea obtained its wine and spirits from smugglers. And this was in spite of a Coastguard station actually on Mersea Hard!

Southend-on-Sea

Southend-on-Sea has by far the largest population of any town in Essex; it covers a vast area, comprising half a dozen once distinct parishes which now merge gently into one another. Much of this development is recent, as is shown by the clear layout of the streets and by the modern commercial centre, particularly the glass-domed Royals Centre for all-weather shopping. Recent improvements in the road links with London mean that the resort is even more accessible to the 20th century visitor.

But this sprawling town had very humble origins: the hamlet of Prittlewell had an ancient Priory, but by the 18th century it was still tiny and occupied only by oystermen working the oyster beds on the foreshore. Then, as the craze for sea bathing began, hotels and boarding houses were built on the cliffs above, including the Grand Hotel

and The Terrace; covered sea water baths were opened, and the Shrubbery was laid out. The resort was patronised in 1803 by Caroline, Princess of Wales, and her 3 month visit did much to enhance the reputation of Southend as a fashionable resort for both Londoners and Essex county families. Disraeli reported that Southend was 'very pretty . . . you could not have a softer climate or sunnier skies'. The rail link from London, only 42 miles distant, was completed in the 1850s.

There are 7 miles of beach, stretching from Leigh-on-Sea to East Beach at Shoebury; but the principal attraction is inevitably the pier, at 2360 yards reputedly the longest in the world. The present construction is about a hundred years old, stretching out into the deeper water to allow access for the steam boats from London. At one time horse drawn trams would meet the passengers at the end of the pier, and carry them to the town. Today's visitor can enjoy a unique ride on the railway which now runs the length of this extraordinary jetty.

There is much to occupy the visitor, both young and old: funfairs, the illuminations, a planetarium, a roller skating rink and a Marine Activity Centre; pretty gardens on the cliffs and at Priory Park; local ice cream and the traditional cockle teas; festivals, both of the Arts and Floral, Europe's biggest Air Show and the annual Sailing Barge Race. If you are seeking entertainment, you need look no further; the motto of Southend-on-Sea seems to be 'Come for the day . . . Stay 'til tomorrow!'

Paycocke's House, Coggeshall

Paycocke's House in Coggeshall's West Street is one of the finest houses in Essex. It was begun in 1500 by John Paycocke, a wealthy local merchant, and completed after his death by his son Thomas. Although the front of the house is justly famous for its exquisite combination of timber, glass and brick, the Paycockes would barely recognise it, as it is the result of recent improvements. The rear of the house is more authentic, and the impression it gives is of haphazard construction, to produce store rooms, work shops and domestic living spaces.

The most extraordinary fact about the present house is that it came very close to being demolished about a hundred years ago! During the 19th century it had been split into three tenements, and by 1890 it had become so grim that it was sold for demolition, with the main timbers destined for other houses. Fortunately, this fate was averted by the actions of local protesters, and the house was bought by Lord Buxton who restored it to its present condition. He is responsible for the beautiful windows and the interesting carved figures either side of the great front doorway. In 1924 Paycocke's became the property of the National Trust.

The interior has obviously undergone enormous changes over the years, but the blending of old and not so old is skilfully effected, and the house still has many features of exceptional quality. The dining room fireplace and the linen-fold panelling date from Tudor times, and the staircase and mullioned windows do not betray their youth. There is a display of lace in one of the rooms, a reminder of one of Coggeshall's chief industries and the source of much of Paycocke's wealth. Originally the garden would have been used for tentering – stretching out cloth for drying – but now it is the epitome of the English country garden with flower beds and lawns which scarcely suggest the hard work put in by the present residents. It is a key factor in the appeal of this property that it has that lived-in feeling.

The town is well worth a visit, and preferably on foot. There are whole streets of pretty houses and shops, and nowadays many of them are crammed with antiques and works of fine art. Market Hill is dominated by the clock tower which commemorates the Jubilee of Queen Victoria. Church Street is delightfully haphazard in its range of buildings, and at the end stands the Woolpack Hotel, a 15th century timber tribute to the pleasures of the palate.

Bradwell on Sea

The walk to the chapel of St Peter on the Wall is delightful. The coastline is low and marshy, with the expanse of the Blackwater estuary passing imperceptibly into the North Sea. The Romans came here first, using Kentish stone to build one of their great Saxon Shore Forts, which in this case was intended to protect their settlements, including Colchester, from the attacks of the raiding Saxons. They called their fort Othona, and while most of it is now beneath the sea, there are some pieces of wall remaining beneath the grass which covers the site. At last the soldiers were withdrawn, and the East Saxons settled down as farmers, and the name of their territory survives as Essex.

Although the Saxons were pagan, their king, Sigbert, wanted to see them converted so he sent into Northumbria for a missionary, and received St Cedd. In AD 653 this first Bishop of Essex arrived by boat, stepping on to the jetty which had once served the Roman fort. He chose to begin his task where he stood: against one of the walls, and using the ample supplies of stone available, he built his cathedral – St Peter on the Wall. Even when it had the rounded apse whose outline is marked in the grass, it was still a very small building; but it served its purpose, and the conversion of East Anglia proceeded.

The path to the chapel is still known as the Pilgrim Way, a reminder of the thousands of people over the centuries who walked to this earliest centre of Christian worship. St Peter's was abandoned in the 17th century, and for a long time served as a barn, but in 1920 it was restored, and today is still in use as a nondenominational chapel. There are regular services during the summer months. The interior is dark and simply furnished, with displays to inform the visitor. The walk is always invigorating, whatever the weather, and the modern world with its cities and motorways could not seem further away or less relevant.

Most of the surrounding marshes have long been drained, and the fields stretch away in unbroken carpets of green or gold, depending on the season. The shoreline here is in the care of the Wildlife Trust, and is used by birdwatchers, and they are responsible for the rather mysterious, tent-like objects which dot the marshes. The most intrusive element of progress is the bulk of the Nuclear Power Station, which by all accounts is likely to last as long as St Cedd's tiny chapel, but with a less agreeable effect on the scenery. In a region famous for its magnificent churches, it is humbling to think that this chapel was the very first.

Walton-on-the-Naze & Frinton

The end of the Georgian period saw the development of Walton-on-the-Naze as a favoured watering place for fashionable Londoners. At this time it was still a village; genteel terraced houses were erected near the front, bathing machines were set up on the beach, and the first hotel, the Portobello, was opened in 1829. The branch line to Walton from the main railway between London and Colchester was opened in 1867, so the town's prosperity dates largely from that time. It is a tribute to Walton that, not only has it used its development wisely to cater in all important ways for the modern tourist, but that it manages to retain that air of elegance which must have attracted visitors a century and more ago.

The main asset is, of course, the beach, which is made up of smooth sand – an enormous expanse of it at low tide, and very safe for children. There is a long pier, but it is used as much by fishermen as by those enjoying the rides, slot machines and tenpin bowling, and it provides a mooring for the Walton and Frinton Lifeboat.

Simple but elegant boarding houses sweep down to the main part of the town with its narrow streets and old-fashioned shops; then there is an immense green area with a children's playground and plenty of room for picnics, and an ultramodern leisure swimming pool. Further along is the old Lifeboat Station, now a small museum dealing with local history. To the north, the ground rises 70 feet to the Naze, a bold promontory crowned by an octagonal brick tower, built in the 18th century to guide mariners safely through the waters. The 137 acres of grassland on the Naze are home to butterflies and moths (such as the Essex Skipper and the rare Emperor moth) and landing point for many birds.

Frinton, lying between Clacton and Walton, is different from these, as the visitor will immediately determine. The town lacks the traditional seaside attractions and works hard to preserve its aloofness. The town gates are known locally as the Heavenly Gates, and those who live inside these gates are considered to be sublimely blessed, for the place is undoubtedly beautiful : neat and attractive, with superbly kept gardens in wide avenues, and small, exclusive shops – Connaught Avenue has earned the name 'the Bond Street of the East Coast'. The beach with its long promenade is reached after a steep walk down the cliffs from the Greensward, an open area of grass overlooked only by gracious flats and small hotels. For those able to forgo man-made amenities and wishing to enjoy a tranquil day of sitting and watching the sky and the sea, there could be no better place.

Mountfitchet Castle

In the famous year of 1066 the Norman baron Robert Gernon, Duke of Boulogne, came to this spot, and built a timber motte and bailey castle. Later it was replaced by one of stone, but it did not last long, for King John ordered it to be levelled, and as Richard de Mountfitchet at the time of his death in 1258 was unmarried and so without a son and heir the castle was left to the weeds, and to anyone in search of stone for building. It became 'The Castle Time Forgot'.

Quite recently, Mountfitchet Castle has been at the centre of a most remarkable act of restoration. Because it is a protected Historic Monument it cannot be dug up or altered, but the new owner wanted to present it to the public as it might have been in its heyday. How could it be done?

Careful research produced an outline of the original pallisade, which would have comprised oak timbers sunk into the rampart. Unable to repeat this technique because it would have involved disturbing the historical evidence, the new castle builders ingeniously stood key timbers in concrete sleepers, which in turn support the full timber defensive line. It is most convincing.

Although the site is on the edge of the village, modern life is easily ignored, as the castle pallisade encircles a grassy mound, itself surrounded by a ditch. Animals and medieval farm tools are in evidence, but they are rather dwarfed by an imposing siege tower, which can offer the energetic visitor an attacker's eye-view of the entire castle layout.

The bailey is an informative area. The life of a castle was centred around farmyard activities for most of the time, and so there are friendly animals wherever you go, and barns waiting to be discovered. A small pond is home to assorted ducks, and chickens scatter in all directions at the least sign of disturbance. Woodsmoke permeates all the buildings and contributes to the impression that this really is an experience in time-travelling. The life-sized model people are very realistic, and can be quite confusing if there are a lot of 20th century visitors, too. Tape recorded commentaries are activated by the visitor at each place, although they fail to wake the drunkard asleep in the pig sty! The Norman lord himself is apparently the guide, and the standard of information supplied is very thorough. The Church is a simple thatched log building, the interior decorated with murals, while outside in the small graveyard lie victims of 'recent' Viking raids, and even the grave of someone killed by a wolf. Weapons of war are ready for immediate action, and in the inner bailey stands the Hall. Once the time-traveller's eyes have adjusted to the smoke-filled gloom it comes as a shock to discover the entire family at table, ready to eat. This may give the impression of being the family house, but in reality it is the last refuge, complete with armoury, tower and watchful sentries.

The rediscovery of Mountfitchet Castle is a piece of good fortune, for it provides a fascinating insight to a vanished period of history without in any way disturbing it.

Dengie Marshes

The Dengie Hundred is a peninsula bounded to the north by the Blackwater and to the south by the Crouch. It is said that the men of Dengie Marshes used to fetch their wives from the uplands, but these poor women lasted 6 months or a year at the most before they succumbed to marsh fever and died. So it was common to have had as many as ten wives – or perhaps more!

Although there is something melancholy, even awesome about mile upon mile of salt water reeds and marshland, the results of progress have proved to be less impressive. Today's Marshes are drained by long ditches, and instead of solitary wildfowl noisily taking flight, there are lone tractors, spluttering their way to the horizon, gouging furrows in the soil. The roads leading east of villages like Asheldham, Southminster and Burnham itself, set off as though determined to arrive, but as the miles pass, they narrow, acquire ever more crippling ruts and bumps until they simply give up and, exhausted, become a farm yard, with nowhere else to go. There are some attractive pubs in the area, and they are friendly and welcoming. A number are fortunate to have gained favourable mentions in respected pub guides.

There is a sort of progress here, for the mighty North Sea has been held at bay, if not tamed, and where once there was wilderness, now the land yields plenty. However, there is always the unsettling feeling that time is not on the side of the forces of order. Although the coast path offers a glimpse of the remaining marshland, the walker must be fit and confident, for between Burnham and Bradwell, many miles to the north, there are few points where the path can be left.

Dengie Flats are all that remain of the once great expanse of saltings which dominated this tongue of land. Now they are reduced to a collar of brown marsh which is unable to penetrate the lush green of the man-made banks upon which the footpath relies for safety. But the song birds remain, offering to the visitor a concerto of perfect sounds, with one instrument taking off when another has paused. The sea wall is a place of beauty and for reflection. Enjoy the eternal simplicity of the coastline, listen to the song of the birds, feel the wind off the grey North Sea, then turn inland to the silent, tamed, exploited farmland: to do so is to confront the true meaning of progress.

Greensted Saxon Church

Two centuries before the Battle of Hastings this church was built! Obviously only parts of it survive from that time, but it is still an extraordinary span of time. Greensted means forest clearing, and once this whole area of Essex was one vast source of mature timber. Today the church of St Andrew is surrounded by pleasant farming country, and the woods have withdrawn to Epping.

St Cedd was a Saxon monk who came to this place in the middle of the 7th century. Nothing of his building remains above ground, but the present walls probably continue the construction techniques he used. The walls are formed by split logs, grooved into each other, and slotted into a base which was once also timber. There was, of course, no shortage of building material! Even the roof would have been formed by split timbers. The interior would have been candle lit for there is no evidence of windows in the early church. The north side provides the best opportunity to see the earliest surviving stretches of log wall. Recent dry summers have caused the timbers to warp, and gaps have appeared which require expensive attention.

Of course, there have been many changes since, for only the central section is of log construction. The brick chancel dates from Tudor times, and the attractive wooden bell tower, with its Essex weatherboarding, may have been built in the following century.

St Edmund was killed by the Danes in AD 870, and his body was taken to Bury St Edmunds in Suffolk. On the way, it rested in this church, an event commemorated by a stained glass window, and a fine carved beam just inside the doorway. Legend claims that the covers of the Bible and Prayer Book are made from the tree he was placed against when the Danes fired arrows into his body, before they beheaded him.

This is still very much a place of worship, with colourful locally made hassocks, and the interior is welcoming and busy, with lots of souvenirs to encourage you to contribute to the next thousand years' upkeep.

Stour Valley

A warm summer's day, with a light breeze ruffling green leaves and blowing little clouds across an otherwise perfect blue sky . . . a peaceful river slipping quietly between the meadows of a fertile valley . . . the age old tower of a church rising above the trees. . . . To many, these scenes are the very epitome of the English countryside; and we owe this vision largely to the extraordinary brilliance of John Constable, who was born in this valley, and whose talent to capture it on canvas has enthralled us all with a view of the ideal.

The River Stour forms the border between Essex and Suffolk, and John Constable was born on the Suffolk side in 1776; he lived his early years at East Bergholt. He attended the Grammar School at Dedham, so every school day would see him walking along these river banks and crossing the Stour. It was a place which he loved beyond all other, and to which he would always return during the summer when, sketchbook in hand, he would walk the meadows and note down the scenes which he would work up into grand paintings during the winter months spent in London, ready for the Exhibition at the Royal Academy the following May.

We should remember, however, that this landscape, so empty and peaceful to us, was a landscape full of incident in days gone by. Golding Constable, John's father, owned Flatford Mill and Dedham Mill and two windmills besides, and for a time it was thought that John would follow in his father's footsteps. These mills, sources of nostalgic interest for us now, were central to industrial life. The River Stour must always have been busy; it was an important highway for all sorts of river traffic, carrying cargoes such as grain and textiles. Golding Constable owned barges which could travel as far inland as Sudbury, once the Stour Navigation canal had been completed in the early 1700s. To be sure, the pace was more leisured than our road and rail traffic nowadays, but it was nevertheless an intrinsic part of industrialised Britain.

Now that the river has been left behind by the demands of progress, we see it more clearly as a part of the rural landscape which offers us recreation; you can hire rowing boats at Dedham or at Flatford Mill, a mile or two downstream, and enjoy a leisurely trip accompanied only by ducks. The National Trust has acquired much of this part of the valley, and a walk along the riverside path is always pleasurable, with the cows chewing solemnly in the fields and the fishermen placidly awaiting their catch. And you are very likely to see an artist, following in the tradition of John Constable, and trying to set down in paint the beauty of this area, still known to us – as it was in the artist's lifetime – as 'Constable Country'.

Basildon

Basildon is a New Town, one of eight sites selected outside the London green belt in the years immediately after the Second World War; it was expected to attract large numbers of Londoners who would become, not simply commuters, but members of a new community. Imagine being asked to create a town from nothing: where would you begin? Even while the construction work is proceeding, your problems are arriving: houses, schools and shops must be available for the first inhabitants, increasing to meet the demands of a growing population – a population which now totals over 150,000.

It is now so well established that we may find it hard to think of Basildon as a New Town. In the early 19th century before the railway line arrived the inhabitants numbered a mere 200! Less than 50 years ago it was, by all accounts, a rather sad part of the county, lacking any sense of purpose, and was even described as a collection of shacks; a rustic slum! Those are probably rather harsh verdicts, as parts of the old Basildon survive. Of particular note is Holy Cross Church. This is a fine building, cheek by jowl with more modern creations, but managing to look good even though parts of it are 600 years old.

Of course, now the town has fine modern buildings, and the street plan is wide and designed to make shopping easy and pleasurable. From the beginning traffic was to be kept in its place, and this has been tackled very successfully. Even in the centre the roads are never too far away, but pedestrians have priority. The feel of the town is friendly and spacious.

At the hub of the ten self contained neighbourhoods which make up the town is the Town Square, which acts as a focal point for the community. This is dominated by Brook House, a 14 storey block of flats which is bravely positioned on 8 triangular legs, each 27 feet high, and splayed out in V shapes. Even the windows of this building are triangular. Around it on two levels is a paved shopping area, enlivened by a long waterway which acts partly as an architectural feature and partly as a display area for modern sculptures. These include a vivid depiction of a mother playing with her child. Everywhere there are shops and amenities to discover, and it is a place for pedestrians to relax and regain their strength.

Close by is the Eastgate Centre, which has four floors crammed with shops of all sorts, including galleries, purveyors of delicious snacks, and pretty flower stalls. It is a high-tech world of glass and moving staircases, conveying shoppers to stores whose names are household words. Cleverly, the conversation piece at the hub of this exciting complex is an eccentric water clock, comprising wheels, wires and even glistening sailing ships, which takes up masses of space from floor to ceiling and demands that it be studied, if only to learn the correct time! At any time of the day it is the perfect meeting place, and waiting becomes fun.

Mistley

What first strikes you about Mistley is not just its pretty riverside setting, with the Stour broadening to about a mile, and the lazy water slipping between mudflats, but the smell of malt lingering heavily in the air. For this is the industry of Mistley, established two centuries ago by a local landowner.

Mistley may still be called an industrialised village, and its quayside has seen a great deal of activity in past years. Its heyday began in the early 1700s, when the building of the Stour Navigation with its 15 locks enabled shipping to penetrate as far inland as Sudbury. The swing of the main channel to the south here enabled quite large vessels to tie up at Mistley Quay.

An associated industry was shipbuilding, principally of sailing barges. These were used to transport the grain on to the lighters which would then take it inland to the mills, and return laden with flour. Constable shows such a barge under construction in his father's dry dock in his painting

Boat building. Prosperity was short-lived; by the mid 19th century, the railway could handle cargoes much more quickly, and although there was a great deal of local opposition from the 'lumpers' or longshoremen, who in one quarrel attacked the railway navvies – and won – the railway eventually prevailed.

But the village did not die, and its survival owes something to the plans of a local landowner. Richard Rigby was a draper's son who made a fortune through his investments. He owned Mistley Hall, and developed the village by setting up on the quayside the granaries and warehouses necessary to enhance the port, and by building malthouses. On the malting house floor, barley was spread out and left to germinate, when it was used in the brewing industry. Nowadays the process has been mechanised, and the premises have moved up the hill, away from the quayside, but the distinctive smell lingers on. The industry had an interesting consequence, since its by products attracted swans which still throng the river in their hundreds. Indeed, the swan has become Mistley's trade mark and the main square of Mistley has an oval pool with a proud swan sitting in the middle. A spring on the hill side above the village used to feed the fountain of water which streamed from the swan's beak. This unusual pool was built by Richard Rigby the younger who inherited his father's wealth and ambitions. This Rigby, an MP, was appointed Paymaster General to the Armed Forces of George III, a lucrative post.

Brentwood

Brentwood is on the very periphery of London – a dormitory town ever since the coming of the railway in the mid 18th century. The spread of London had begun even earlier, and nowadays it is difficult to see where Essex ends and Greater London begins.

The town was originally a ribbon development on the old Roman Road. It was this route that pilgrims from East Anglia had used when travelling through the capital and thence to the shrine of St Thomas a Becket at Canterbury. Brentwood was ideally placed as a stopping point for travellers, and there are reminders of this: some of the oldest inns survive, including the White Hart which has an inner coaching yard and gallery, and at nearby Mountnessing the Prince of Wales has a list of tolls charged at the tollgate on the Great London Road.

The centre of Brentwood has some interesting features. Firstly there are the ruins of the 13th century chapel dedicated to St Thomas of Canterbury; only two of the walls and part of a tower survive, but the area has been planted with flowers and it points a pleasing contrast with the nearby Chapel High shopping precinct, with all its modernity.

The second notable monument is to be found at Wilson's Corner, at the crossroads with the Shenfield Road. Here is a granite obelisk, erected in 1861 to the memory of a local martyr, William Hunter.

The tree at which Hunter was burned was moved from its original position in Ingrave Road to Brentwood School museum; the obelisk was severely damaged in a great fire in the early 1900s, and despite restoration, the cracks caused by the intense heat of the fire – which destroyed Wilson's draper's store – may still be seen.

In recent years the town has been bypassed, but the centre still hums with a constant stream of traffic, and the many modern businesses attract a large number of shoppers.

Nearby Mountnessing has a fine 300 years old post mill. This was restored in 1935 by the local parish council to celebrate the Jubilee of George V. It stands at the northern end of the town, just off the main road, and surrounded by fields. You cannot miss it!

Tilbury Fort

Almost the last thing the visitor to this part of the country expects to find is a piece of history, because the banks of the Thames are changing at a great rate, and the last century has not been kind to this part of Essex. However, it is perhaps a tribute to the builders of the distant past that their work has survived upheaval, enemy bombs and even the assaults of developers. Tilbury Fort stands today a unique reminder of London's maritime importance, and as such it is well worth a visit.

The most famous event connected with this place is the moment in 1588 when as England trembled at the prospect of invasion by the Spanish Armada, Queen Elizabeth rode to Tilbury to inspect her troops, and assured them that she would lead them to victory. So she did, but nothing of that fort remains.

The fort we see today dates from the time of Charles II, and is the best example of its type. In the mid 17th century England found itself at war with the naval power of the Dutch, and the fear was that a fleet would sail up the Thames and cause havoc in England's busiest waters. Tilbury Fort was designed by the Dutchman Sir Bernard de Gomme to contain great guns which would inflict certain destruction on any fleet foolhardy enough to engage its batteries. De Gomme's nationality was not allowed to be a problem. To ensure the safety of the fort itself, enormous bastions of brick were constructed following the plan of a regular pentagon. The Water Gate is very grand, and bears an inscription to Charles II. Two encircling moats were dug which would deter even the most desperate of land attacks. The ingenuity of de Gomme even included planning for the eventuality of the moat icing over – sluices enabled the water to be drained, leaving a formidable ditch! Today there are splendid wooden drawbridges to be seen. As with many great military schemes the test never came, and the only occasion when the fort fired its guns in anger was much later, during the First World War, and then the enemy was flying overhead. A Zeppelin was shot down. The parade has an area of two and a half acres and encloses impressive barrack blocks, and partially concealed magazines.

Today the Fort offers a wonderful vantage point from which to enjoy the River Thames, and a modern promenade and river wall outside enable you to benefit from the fresh air which is a feature of this vantage point. The pub nearby is called The World's End, and was once the old ferry house. It is a delightful timber building and just the place to reflect on all the history which has flowed past its door.

Epping & Hatfield Forests

Up until Norman times, most of Essex was covered by a dense forest, the hunting ground of kings. What remains today, though only a fraction of the original, shows us beautiful green places, so close in terms of miles to the capital, but so far from it in their tranquil atmosphere.

Epping Forest covers a long crescent of 6000 acres of land, much of it bordered by densely populated areas. There are traces of its earlier history. Iron Age earthworks at Ambresbury Bank are reputed to be the site of Boudicca's last hopeless stand against the Romans. At Chingford there is an interesting timber framed hunting lodge built by Henry VIII, where Elizabeth I is said to have rode up and down the stairs on her horse! Later, the town of Epping – a mile long, and cushioned from the overspill of London by the protective forest – was an important staging post on the London

Road, its 16 inns offering a last stop before the depths of the Forest, where highwaymen such as the infamous Dick Turpin might spring from their lairs and prey on unsuspecting travellers. Epping Forest might so easily have been broken up and lost to us as other Royal Forests (such as Hainault Forest) were. But after a protracted legal battle, the citizens of Epping forced the protection of the forest with a parliamentary Act of 1878. To signal this definitive halt to the development of London, Queen Victoria officially opened the Forest to public access in 1882. Since then, strenuous efforts have been made to preserve the ancient woodland and grassland, and the Conservation Centre at High Beach tells the full story. A third of the area is used for grazing; the rest is a mixed woodland of oak, hornbeam and beech, home to a wide range of birds and animals.

Hatfield Forest is much smaller (1049 acres) and lies near the recently extended Stansted Airport, bounded on the north by the A120 road. This Forest was saved in 1923. The owners, the Houblon family, had brought in a timber merchant to fell it, but it was bought by Edward North Buxton who died the following year, leaving the Forest to the National Trust.

Access to the Forests is easy, and in parts they have a suburban feel; but a visit in spring when the new leaves are unfolding, or in autumn when a carpet of fallen leaves covers the forest floor with gold, is a tonic for visitors from town and countryside alike.

Wivenhoe

The River Colne may not be the longest or busiest river in East Anglia, but it is surely one of the prettiest. It flows from Colchester into the River Blackwater, and the point where it passes Mersea Island is famous for the oyster beds which continue an association stretching back to Roman times. Fingringhoe Creek is still known as the Roman River.

Half way down the River Colne stands Wivenhoe, a pretty port. From the river it is seen at its best, as a row of soft coloured houses jostle to retain a waterfront position. In the centre of the quay stands the Rose and Crown, brightly clad in a primrose wash, and the centre of activity at the end of the day. Behind it, the 15th century tower of St Mary the Virgin is crowned with an unusual cupola, and completes a perfectly proportioned scene. Scores of sailing craft are tied up to the quayside, and even manage to please the eye when dried out, the yachtsman's euphemism for high and dry, and surrounded by mud!

Wivenhoe has been a bustling port and centre for ship building for centuries, but it was the Victorians who gave it a new lease of life. Today there are cargo wharves upstream, handling timber and coal, and a continued interest in the traditional craft of clinker construction sailing boats.

Close by Anchor Hill, which is the centre of the town, stands the Garrison House. This is distinguished by an upper storey of exquisite 17th century pargeting, where plasterwork is embellished with intricate designs and patterns. In this case there is a wealth of scrolls and leaves. It is thought that Cromwell stayed here, so possibly he was among the first to marvel at the effect!

In April 1884 this quiet town was rocked by the Colchester earthquake. This unusual occurrence was serious, destroying or damaging 200 buildings. The church was very badly affected, and had to be largely rebuilt. One of the Quayside cottages, which needed restoration, displays the date of the event.

Wivenhoe Park was purchased by Essex County Council in 1962, and in time became the University of Essex. The conversation overheard outside the Rose and Crown or the equally agreeable Black Buoy may be surprisingly academic or ribald.